MW01273762

THE
INDEPENDENT
ELDERLY

Tips for Caring Family & Friends

———

Relta M. Gray

CLASSIC DAY
PUBLISHING

Seattle, Washington
Portland, Oregon
Denver, Colorado
Vancouver, B.C.
Scottsdale, Arizona
Minneapolis, Minnesota

Classic Day Publishing
2925 Fairview Avenue East
Seattle, Washington 98102
877-728-8837
info@peanutbutterpublishing.com

Acknowledgements

—◦∾◦—

In grateful acknowledgement of the advice, encouragement, support and cautions to Keith Ly, DO; Franco Bacerdo, DPM; Scott Campbell, OD; Wayne C. McCormick, MD, MPH; Reverend William McKee, several geriatric therapists, the Lunch Bunch, the pinochle group, many friends and family who shared experiences, and especially to my granddaughter, Kara McGinn, who not only literally saved my life by knowing the Heimlich Maneuver, but has served as primary editor and lay-out artist for this little book.

The Independent Elderly

—◦◦◦—

This little book has been written on behalf of all the independent elderly, defined as those individuals living alone, by choice or by other circumstances. It is intended for caring family and friends who do not always understand the desire to remain independent as long as possible. It will, hopefully, lead to the understanding of distinction between actively caring about, and providing care for, older family and friends.

Table of Contents

—⟶∿∿⟵—

Who Am I?

—ᷣᵥᵥᷣ—

Speaking for this group of independent people (being one myself), we are convinced in many cases that we can take care of ourselves. Remember that some of us will reach 100 easily. There are others who need assistance in many small ways so that they can continue being an independent person. We are often a problem. We find it difficult to ask for even a little help, find it hard to say "please," and hide our needs away until they become a necessity. We tend to cover up and, yes, to fudge the truth a bit.

These independent people, living alone, are a very real concern for families in particular. Many do not see each other on a daily basis. It is more likely to be a weekly occurrence. Daily phone calls often avoid discussions of any need. We hope the cautions detailed here will help both the independent elder as well as caring family and friends.

I'd like to explain how I became an "expert" on the subject. Some of it is very personal and some came from my doctor and my pastor, from professional caregivers and geriatric specialists. Many were observations and complaints given freely by friends and associates. A good share came from my monthly card club – eight good women, the youngest of whom is 75. Then there is the "Lunch Bunch," a group of 24 women meeting for more than forty years of monthly luncheons, down to only ten of us now, and the youngest is also 75. All have common complaints and/or questions. I am the oldest at both my monthly meetings. I find that 90 years has settled rather comfortably on my shoulders in spite of all the things attached to old age. I never expected to see the year 2000 arrive but here I am at the year 2006! From these resources a simple, rather down-to-earth list has evolved.

It was my good fortune to have had a lifetime in a professional position that was my dream from high school. It was work that I reluctantly gave up as age began to creep up. It was in the year 2000, at the age of 85, that full-time employment was relinquished, but I continued to work part-time until November 2004 when the final tie to the office was cut. I have been most fortunate. Through the aging process, I found myself with time on my hands and wondering what lay ahead. It has been this evolution of life that has brought me to the desire to share my thoughts on aging with others.

I would like to examine some of the problems that arise with aging, and how caregivers can recognize signs of need. Along with that I have made a few suggestions as to the best way to approach these issues.

Fear and Frustration

Fear is the paramount word in the senior category. We are afraid of a crippling illness occurring. We are scared to death of falling and being wheelchair bound. We worry about a place to live and are fearful that it will be a nursing home situation. If we live too long, what will happen to us financially? We don't want to be a charity case, or forced to live with a family member who doesn't really want us but feels obligated for our care. If we live in another city or state, will we be taken from our familiar spaces and transported so that our care will be simpler for the family?

Fears bring on frustrations. We do not want to become a burden to family. We don't want to give up all our independence and we haven't yet figured out how to retain it. We begin to feel like a baby who needs constant care. We know that isn't really true but it feels so because we haven't learned how to say "no" and sometimes "yes" easily. We haven't been schooled in asking for help and how to accept it when given.

Our Bodies, Ourselves

As we age, we find changes occurring in our body; in fact, our whole well-being. Not everyone experiences the same changes and, in some, they do not occur to a great extent. We notice that our bones become more brittle, that our skin tends to dry out, eating habits change, dexterity and stance are at risk.

All this begins with our five senses, which affect all of our health changes. Special attention must be given to our sight, hearing, smell, taste and touch. Let's begin with an overview of each of these areas.

An Overview of the Senses

―∾∿∾―

Sight

Deterioration may not be so recognizable in those who have worn glasses for some time. There are some indica- tions that changes are occur- ring when it becomes appar-
ent that large print type is better, a chair is positioned closer to the TV screen, dust goes unnoticed, and even an unexpected choice of clothing for the day brings comments and concerns.

Hearing

This loss appears to be more gradual, and is often denied. Again, the need for increase in sound volume of any kind – speaking, TV or music, other entertainment forms, becomes a cause for concern. A reminder that fire alarms and smoke detectors fall into this category. Also, dizziness or light-headed experiences can indicate inner ear problems.

Smell

This is a very personal situation often not readily recognized by those who are aging and certainly not by those caring for them. It is often a gradual loss. Because it is so personal, it can be anything from a pan left to burn on the stove, too much cologne or aftershave, a matter of personal cleanliness, or an unnoticed odor in an area such as a bathroom or kitchen.

Taste

This is also in the personal category since every person has different likes and dislikes. It becomes crucial where diets are concerned, eating habits are affected and, in some cases, where medications are involved. It often is a reason for our menu choices. We may not notice if food has spoiled, so take care to show us how to check for expiration dates on meats especially.

Touch

This involves dexterity of fingers and hands, foot movement, caresses, physical ailments, any personal contacts. There are many signs to watch for as we age: loss of strength, problems with opening jars and pill bottles, handling heavy or awkward objects, dealing with buttons and zippers, etc. In following segments of this book, other indications are noted pertaining especially to strength-loss issues.

A List of Tips, Alphabetically

—◆◆◆—

Before I begin with some thoughts on how to observe and help your loved ones, I ask that you remember, first of all, that COMMON SENSE is the one factor that governs all decisions. And, secondly, remember to help us preserve our dignity and pride along the way.

A cautionary note: all things do not necessarily apply to every person. While aches and pains assail all of us, the remedies vary from person to person. Every solution can be different depending upon health, attitude, and, of course, finances.

Autos, Vans

Do I know the proper way to get into and out of a vehicle?

In a passenger car, and even getting into a van where step stools are used, the instructions are the same. When in position, back up to the seat, sit down, turn slightly, and then swing both legs into the car. Be sure hands are free. Many cars and vans have hand holds that, in most cases, are helpful in settling into the seat.

Since curbs have a tendency to vary in height, it is often better when exiting a car, to have the driver stop far enough from the curb so that feet can be planted firmly on the ground. There is no graceful way to exit a car, but this does help: the rider can then turn and swing his/her legs into the street. Stepping up on to the curb is not as difficult as trying to place feet firmly on a space that is often too high or too small to get good traction.

———✳———

Bathing/Showers

Am I safe?

For those who have had daily baths or showers, it often becomes a daunting task since it is not only tiring, but a bit scary as well. So we begin to limit the frequency with which we bathe.

Actual tub baths are never advised unless immediate assistance is at hand. Getting in and out of the tub is a hazard in itself. The dangers in a bathroom are discussed under the topic of **Safety Hazards** but bear repeating since falls occurring in this area are among the most frequent accidents.

Be sure when standing in the tub or shower enclosure that there are safety grooves in the tub or floor area and that mats are non-skid. On the side walls should be properly installed handles to use for balance. Chairs or benches developed for showering permit the use of flexible hand-held devices and allow a good shampoo. If choosing to stand in the shower, avoid shampooing as part of the bathing process and use a sink for shampooing instead. Many shampoos and conditioners have oil bases that can cause slips in a tub. When possible, try to schedule bathing when someone is at hand to assist if needed in getting in and out of the bathing facility.

Buttons & Other Small Objects

Am I struggling to get dressed or open jars?

Loss of dexterity can occur in just the fingers. It is not always attributable to arthritis, although this is certainly true in many instances. Becoming a person with "fumble fingers" is not always reassuring. Watch for the difficulty in trying to fit small buttons into buttonholes, trying to open bottles or pull back tabs on cans, working puzzles, lighting candles, tying shoe laces, trying to pull open the wax paper containers in cereal boxes, all things that require steady and firm fingers. These indications are easily discovered when one is observant.

Zippers may not be the answer, since guiding the fastener into the proper channel is often awkward and frustrating. Changing to larger buttons works for a time, but the shape and the fabric to which buttons are attached sometimes pose additional difficulties. Try buttoning the garment while it is lying flat, leaving enough headroom. Velcro may be the answer for some situations. Pullovers can solve some problems.

A caution about dressing is in order: SIT DOWN when putting on pants, socks and shoes. No hopping around on one foot, grasping for a handhold, while trying to get one foot in a pant leg or a stubborn shoe on a foot. This can be a recipe for disaster.

⟜◦◦◦⟞

Canes & Other Walking Devices

Do I have a safe balancing device?

Sometimes people who find they are having difficulty walking, particularly in balance, arbitrarily start using a cane to help them. In these circumstances, the cane often becomes a hazard instead of a help.

It is imperative that each user be measured for proper height of any walking device. The cane, in particular, if too tall, can tangle the feet and cause falls. The doctor will usually recommend some therapy when it becomes evident that help is needed in walking. This is a great decision, because you learn exactly what to do, how to walk in a straight line, to go up and down stairs. However, as more than one therapist confided, the first trip to the therapy session is often the only time they see the patient. The patient came because the doctor had made the appointment, perhaps, but once they find that it will be at least once a week for a prescribed number of visits, and that instructions will be given for the proper exercises at home that must be performed on a daily basis, they apparently are unwilling to give the time and effort and never return.

Personally, I had the same feeling. But common sense prevailed since I went to the doctor for help in the first place, and if I wasn't willing to go by his direction, then the whole effort was for nothing. It turned my life around, since I learned to negotiate stairs, to walk a straight line on the sidewalk. My cane became my ally. A word of caution about rubber tipped canes: The rubber wears down. Examine the cane tip from time to time. Frequently used on sidewalks, they will wear smooth and may cause one to slip and slide. Replacement tips are available at almost every place foot medications are sold. A little secret about canes as well – they can become an offensive weapon if the need should arise.

"Walkers" pose some of the same difficulties if the right height is not obtained. There is also the right weight and overall size. Have the user-to-be try them out before purchasing. The same advice goes for the small electric carts with shopping bag space. Too often they are overloaded and are hazardous to the user as well as the public.

—◦◦◦—

Caregivers

Are you treating me like a child?

Too many caregivers, in an effort to be sure they are helping, often lean over backwards in shepherding the elderly. They resist letting us walk in certain areas, or they take our elbows to assist in walking or going up and down stairs, which in itself is hazardous. They also try to get us seated as soon as possible, when in truth the elderly like to move around, look at art in a gallery, shake hands at a gathering, be active and participate in events.

Do not banish them as children often are. Just note that we are slower. We do not break easily, so feel free to hug and to touch us.

⟞ⱷⱷⱷ⟝

Choking

Am I having trouble eating?

The causes are varied. As we age, many of our bodily parts age as well. We find that the various parts of the digestive tract are no longer friendly to us. Or, for one reason or another, breathing becomes difficult. If choking occurs, immediately apply the Heimlich Maneuver. When living alone, a person can apply this to their own body by grasping the back of a chair, or whatever is stable and handy and pushing the upper torso area hard against the chair.

Food is the arch enemy of the elderly. Soft breads, meats, grains of rice and nuts are among the worst for those with swallowing problems. Eating too rapidly, talking with food in the mouth, big bites, gulping liquids and not chewing thoroughly are culprits. Coughing is brought on and this is especially dangerous for those with other ailments, such as congestive heart failure. If you have something lodged in your throat and you begin coughing and cannot get it up, you begin to lose your breath and when the blackness approaches, you are at death's door. My granddaughter literally saved my life when I experienced this sensation. Be sure to eat small bites, eat slowly, do not talk while food is in the mouth, sip your beverages, and eat often during the day. Three meals are always recommended but six small ones might be even better for some.

Companionship/Romance

What do I long for?

Don't laugh. For every person who has had a good marriage or a long-term commitment, the loss of that closeness never completely goes away. Time will diminish some of the loss, but the longing remains. It would be nice to have a man – or lady – friend who speaks your language, who remembers the early years and all the experiences we had during those years. We'd like once more to waltz around a floor to one of the hit tunes of the 40's and 50's. It would be nice to walk hand-in-hand around the block or to the park. It would be fun to play a hand of gin rummy or pinochle, or to put together a jigsaw puzzle. We long to have a hug, a kiss, a soft hand on our cheek. Most of us are not thinking of marriage.

Family and friends fill many of the voids, but there is always a little part of the heart that is always searching for a little romance. The flame may dim, but it never dies.

Do you know any lonesome grandmas or grandpas, aunts or uncles? Help us meet each other.

—⁓∽⁓—

Death

Did you ask me how I feel about death?

No one, especially those still facing a long life, wish to look at this. However, the longer we live, the more comfortable we become with facing this final part of our lives. Talk openly with us. Let us express our feelings and our wishes. Ask us to put things in writing in the form of a Living Will. Our desires about being kept on life support if we are ill, if we are organ donors (it is surprising how many of our old parts are still useful), our wishes for the final services and our preferences regarding cremation or burial need to be expressed. This little chore is not only satisfying to us, but we know from many conversations how much family members appreciate being able to follow our wishes without trying at the last minute to think what we would like if we were able to tell you. Putting it in writing is the best we can do *now*.

—⟶∿∿∿⟵—

Depression

Do I seem sad or not myself lately?

This may be indicated in the lowered energy level but it is often difficult to detect. It can take many forms and is especially difficult when older people refuse to acknowledge that it may be occurring. This can arise when a person retires from work, especially after several years at the same job and with no plan for what to do next. Suddenly faced with no good reason to arise at  the same time, getting ready for work, and out the door, what to do? It's hard to know what or where to start the day.

This was my own personal dilemma and it was the doctor who diagnosed this as a form of depression. He revealed that it was a problem the medical profession faced far too often. Since he learned very rapidly that I had not really planned my immediate future, he sat me down for a heart-to-heart discussion. (It would be wonderful if all doctors could spend this time with a patient. Many frustrations and heartbreak could be avoided.) We discussed what my work had been, and he pointed out that I still had the same skills, was still alert enough to be a consultant, to take on one or two marketing clients who knew my work ability and who could be served from home. He told me about a medical tool he had invented and that was now undergoing testing. When completed, he said that if I was interested I could help with the marketing of his product. We both knew that because of testing and research time, I would probably not be around to take on the work. But it was a bolster to my confidence.

Now I was faced with making plans for the future since it seemed that I would be around for some time. I had been fortunate to travel rather extensively in my work life, so travel was not something I longed for. I had to also realize that my income had been cut considerably. I had two immediate things going for me. I played pinochle with a card group once a month, and I had a "lunch bunch" - old friends from my working days - that met once a month for lunch, an event that we have been enjoying for forty or more years. The group has dwindled from 24 to about ten now, with moves and mostly deaths. These two events I am still enjoying, albeit as the oldest in each group. I have also gone onto other things stemming from my work, and am happier and more fulfilled since the retirement than I ever expected to be. I suggest that you take a look at what each retiree has to offer and help them to make use of their talents.

A word of caution: Many are happy to just sit at home and enjoy television or the computer, but activity, both physical and mental, is the key to a healthy, happy life. Encourage volunteerism, but be certain that it is the right venture for each person. Remind them that it need not be an every day chore. A friend, who chose to go into public school and help the younger students with their reading, was totally burned out after two years and was forced to stop. She did find other outlets but found it wise to make commitments only for a certain period of time, stated on the first day of each new venture. Another who was determined to teach an illiterate adult to read received a strong "kibosh" from her family. They pointed out her tendency to start feeling sorry for the student, literally adopting them as family, bringing them home for meals, worrying about their family life, and getting literally so entangled there was no way out. In this case, her family was totally right since she had a history of doing this all her life, and one she clearly recognized.

Find out what interests us. Is it art, music, gardening, books, research, writing, teaching or speaking? Or, consider encouraging them to go back to school, to learn about a special interest such as history or music and so on. Some universities and community colleges offer audit classes to the elderly at no cost or at best, reduced fees as space is available. These are only the beginning. Where to start? Most cities or neighborhoods have senior programs offering suggestions. Look at meeting notices in the local or daily newspaper where meetings or lectures are listed. It is amazing the variety of opportunities available.

There are many ways to volunteer that take perhaps half a day a week, or a few hours on other given days. It is often a case of senior helping senior. It may be through church, school or an organization they first become involved in while still working. Needs are everywhere. Just help them find the right fit and encourage them to do so. Time will never hang heavy on hands when they are occupied.

Driving

What if I still wish to drive?

This is a difficult subject and requires much tact, sensitivity and a whole lot of loving. The car is an old "buddy" and keeps us independent, even if this is the wrong independence sought. For those who have made the decision to stop driving on their own, it was a wise one.

For me, living in a metropolitan city with narrow streets and too many cars, it was a case of fear on my part. I became afraid to drive – afraid that I might kill someone, or myself, or cripple someone, or hit a dog. My driver's license had five years left on it before renewal. The sad part is that friends think I should still be driving. In my head, I agree, but common sense gave me the answer. There are good and careful older people who drive sanely and with no fear.

One of the problems is that everyone thinks they are in the best of health. If they considered how much medication they took each day and what it was prescribed for, perhaps they would understand the wisdom of turning in their keys. Yes, it makes one dependent on other forms of transportation and it takes longer to go anywhere because more time is required to reach a destination. The hardest part is being forced to ask for transportation assistance in getting to doctor appointments, the grocery store, funerals and the whole gamut of living. It is a favor hard to request.

Note the accidents recorded. Many are seniors driving who have had strokes, a heart attack, diabetic blackouts, blurred vision, and who didn't consider they were a hazard on the road. The reactions to a situation that arises on a highway are much slower in the older driver – another hazard. The speed at which cars travel even in-city is very daunting and the young ones who are eager to pass are not polite drivers but will speed up and often illegally pass on the shoulder or swerve into driveways, and so on, just to get around.

There are some plus points to be considered, of course, regarding giving up driving. Car insurance is no longer needed – quite a dollar savings! Also, consider the regular maintenance costs, license fees, taxes and tires… all no longer a worry. Senior fares are offered for most public transportation. Some areas have special access transportation for those unable to drive, also at a reduced rate. We get to visit with friends, grandchildren, sons and daughters, who become our chauffeurs – especially when scheduled in advance.

—◦◦◦—

Eating Habits

Am I having difficulty with certain foods?

There are so many emergencies which occur because of poor eating habits. Talking with a mouth full can bring on choking. This is the most fearful of all. There are other causes of choking. Food is not well chewed and too large or too soft pieces get lodged in the throat. Dentures which do not fit well may cause some of this problem. Meats, grains, nuts and soft breads are among the worst culprits in getting food stuck in the esophagus.

A doctor may recommend that tests be given to see that the esophagus is working correctly. As one ages, muscles have a tendency to relax and food moves too slowly on its way to the digestive tract. Dilation of the esophagus can help. Most medical programs pay for this procedure. I recommend eating slowly, with smaller bites. No need to go to baby food, although there are times one would like to try. Sip drinks slowly since gulping will bring on air which causes water or other beverages to exit through the nose. Sound gross? It also feels that way.

Consider using a smaller dinner plate for meals that are eaten with other people. Put the smaller amounts usually consumed on the plate and almost always, you find that the smaller-plated eater finishes at the same time as the one with a larger plate.

Appetites, for the most part, grow smaller with age. It is to be recommended that three meals are eaten regularly. Sometimes that doesn't work, and five or six smaller ones are the answer. Listen to the doctor's dietary recommendations. For instance, congestive heart problems call for at least three fish entrees per week. Salt and sugar are the enemies and must be closely watched. This does not mean giving up your favorite foods. As one person said, when her sweet tooth starts nagging at her, she makes a batch of chocolate fudge. However, by the time she has licked the spoon and the pan, she is satisfied and gives all the candy away. Or we find that our taste buds aren't what they used to be, and we need tart foods, spicy seasoning, and so on. We all understand this but we also know that a little goes a long way since too much can induce other problems.

———✦✦✦———

Emergency Preparation

Do I have a way to call for help in an emergency?

Have an open discussion with your independent elder regarding how they might handle an emergency if it occurred while they were alone.

Consider a life-saving alert device such as those worn as pendants or wrist packs. If a fall occurs and help is needed, the button can be immediately activated and the person indicated as closest to the scene will be immediately notified. The local emergency units will also be contacted all within a short time. These alerts are available with monthly rates and give loads of peace of mind to family members.

There are many companies who market life saving alerts. Investigate as to how long they have been in business, their reputation and their area of coverage. There are some scams out there, so beware.

If you have had CPR, Heimlich or other life saving training, be sure to know the most current course. Changes take place frequently.

Also, be sure that extra supplies are on hand for power outages: extra blankets, a flashlight with fresh batteries in an easy to reach location, extra pantry supplies, etc. This will go far to alleviate stress levels.

Energy Level

Do I still have my get up and go?

Be aware that as the day progresses, the energy level diminishes. Most of us know that by 3pm we are ready to sit quietly or to nap. If events, such as theater, an afternoon ball game, or other entertainment venues that may extend that time limit, one way or another, the next day will probably need to be a rest day to recoup. Long car rides can result in sleeping instead of viewing. Family gatherings, not to be missed by any means, should not worry anyone if you find us sitting in a corner and observing instead of helping with dishes or the children.

A caution here is to watch for patterns changing. If we tend to sleep or nap all day, a medication change may be in short order or this may be a sign of other issues including depression. Join us at our next doctor visit to discuss our energy level.

Be wary of those of us who may look very energetic on the outside, but are hiding our true energy level so we are not left out of events. It's important to have a frank discussion with us as to how we are really feeling.

—◈◈◈—

Exercise

A nasty word?

To many of those for whom you are caring, exercise would seem a nasty word. It connotes a lot of movement and hard work and we've had our share of that. Listen to a doctor's advice. It may be difficult but most will not prescribe unusually vigorous workouts. They will tell you – WALK – and that may be the most important word in this paragraph. The pace you set or the distance you walk are not the important parts of this exercise. It is getting outside three days or more each week, for at least twenty to thirty minutes. It does mean walking, not finding a convenient spot to sit and watch others walk. Establishing a routine – time of day, route to be walked that day, etc., will make time go fast, and set a pace to keep. You meet so many interesting people along the way - older people who are making daily walks as you are. Lots of smiles are exchanged, words of greetings, conversations and new sidewalk friends are made. Walking not only provides a break in the humdrum day but is a healthy benefit to the body. If you are doing walking while shopping, it can be counted as part of your walking schedule. If a nap is needed upon return, it is okay.

Walking is the number one exercise for the elderly. There are other forms that are good as well, and as mentally fulfilling. If a pool is convenient, daily or weekly swimming is recommended. Many pools offer water exercise. If golf or tennis have been the number one sport, and if walking is okay, there is no reason to give them up. However, the number of holes played, or the number of games on the court, will need to be reduced to accommodate the strength available for the sport. Limit the amount of time so all is not spent on a once-a-week game.

Yoga and other forms of meditation have much to offer in the way of relaxation. I have no experience with any of these but have a great deal of respect for those who favor these practices. Sit down exercises have gained favoritism among those unable to walk. There are classes offered on public television stations. I recently witnessed some wonderful sessions on television and learned that tapes and instructions are available at nominal costs. They permit a person to set their own time schedule. The exercises are all simple and designed for the body. The beauty of this type of exercise is that it can be done while sitting in a chair. It helps to tone the body as well as gives a cardiovascular workout.

The idea of exercise is to keep the body in tune while helping to stimulate the appetite and eat healthy. This keeps the head clear to make decisions, to learn and observe, to help muscles toughen and, as a bonus, helps to control weight.

Eyes

Have you noticed me squinting?

Some of the more noticeable signs of eye problems were touched on in the introductory paragraph on sight. There are, however, some more serious actions to be observed. Any frequent irritation of the eye such as watering, red eyes, dry eyes, rubbing eyes often, and particularly blurred vision, can be indications of help needed for the eyes. They may be a sign of something else awry in the system such as allergies or diabetes, which frequently attacks the eye and can lead to loss of vision. Other indications may be the formation of cataracts, glaucoma or macular degeneration. Eyesight may be a delicate subject and difficult to discuss, but be persistent when you see continuing signs.

—⟋⟍⟍—

Facial Hair

Are people starting to notice?

This is a particular horror for women but may, in some cases, apply also to men. Care must be taken in what is prescribed to solve this situation. Sensitive or dry skin, shaky hands, uncertain vision, can all be hazards. So it behooves the caregiver to be aware of how to help. The wild hair, for instance, that seems to grow one inch or more overnight, is often hard to pull out and will need help. Look for those that show up in the eyebrows or around the chin. Check ears and nose as well. We hate those wild ones and are embarrassed. Women often have "whiskers" growing in the chin area or just above the mouth. If left alone, they will make real goatees.

So what to do? There is, of course, the visit to a dermatologist but most people try remedies at home first. Since dry skin is often a problem, all recommended hair-removal creams and lotions will not work since the strength will cause irritation to the skin. Laser methods have been developed and are successful in most all cases. There has been some progress in developing razors for women that seem to be okay to use. However, avoid shaving, especially with the disposable shavers made for women, since nicks and cuts often occur.

Men will need some of the same remedies since wild hairs don't choose gender when appearing, and often eyebrows need attention. If they grow a beard it may be from choice. Try to ascertain if they are no longer able to really shave themselves so that a beard becomes the easy way out. It may not be the choice they wish to make. Each individual has their own problems and this is meant only as a suggestion to keep your eye on the face of those for whom you are caring.

———◦◦◦———

Gadgets

How difficult are they to use?

Have you seen the latest invention to open jars? How about the one that opens soda cans? While some of the latest gadgets look like they might be helpful for the elderly, be sure the intended recipient can handle whatever the gift may be. Try it out first. See how easy or hard it may be to operate. Keep them simple or you may find the gift sitting idle on a shelf. Be aware of the finger and hand strength of the recipient. Are they destined to be put away and never used? See "Gifts" section in this book for some useful suggestions for this category.

—◈◈—

Gifts

Are they instantly useful or are they destined for the shelf?

These are a few ideas for birthdays, Christmas or other special holidays that may solve wondering as to what to give as a gift. The most important tip is to not just give "stuff"

where there is no space in which to show them off or to store.

Photos

Always welcome. However, where do they go once given? For those living in restricted units, it is often hard to find a good display area. Perhaps putting together a montage of photos and having them framed would solve that problem since wall space is usually available. Putting a photo album together for us is always appreciated!

Clothing

While always welcome, sometimes it is a treat to do the shopping ourselves. This speaks to gift certificates. When gifting with various pieces of clothing, remember that jackets, cardigan sweaters and pants, should all have pockets. Remember the admonitions above about buttons, zippers, Velcro and pullovers. Bright colors go well with old age. Just be sure they are acceptable and enhancing to the recipient. Do remember that shopping trips are often fun but limit the time spent. It is wearing trying on clothes.

Sports fan?

Treat this person to a couple of tickets to a game of one of the local teams. Being accompanied by a grandson or nephew is a special treat. Remember that afternoon games are probably best and allow time for our slow progress to get to the seats.

Jewelry

Men and women all are intrigued with looking good. Just be sure that whatever the choice is that each one is easy to put on, to fasten, to wind, to pin in place, and so on. This is one of the "fumble fingers" cautions.

The Sweet Tooth

Care must be taken with the health of the recipient. If being treated for some health problem, then abide by the directions given for the ailment. There is a bright spot, however. Since so much attention has been given to this problem in recent years, many new products are now available including sugar-free candy, cookies, and other delicacies. Do a little research. It will be a real treat.

Newspapers, Magazines, Books

If they enjoy a daily newspaper or a special magazine, this is a great gift. Reduced incomes often preclude such subscriptions. Books can be new, thrift store, or exchanges with other readers. Ascertain if public libraries are available near their home. Large print has been a boon to the older vision. Many will protest that it is not needed, but try a sample or two on them. It encourages reading. A wide variety of books are offered in large print as well as magazine versions of many well known publications.

Magnifying Devices

These are a handy-dandy little tool since they are available in many sizes and strengths. Some are sized to fit a full page in a book. The magnification helps in small print, such as on medication containers, recipes or telephone books.

Games

This gives a wide choice since the recipient may have certain things they particularly enjoy. Jigsaw puzzles seem to be a favorite since they can be left out and worked at leisure. Playing cards are a good choice. Just don't give new decks every year. They don't wear out that fast! Also there are several choices for card holders for those who have difficulty with the number of cards held in the hand. Another idea is a card shuffler. Board games, such as Monopoly and Clue, are popular. Cribbage, checkers, dominoes and chess may be games played in earlier years and now there is time to become more proficient. Many will enjoy the games played on TV. However, since most games involve other people, board games and cards are recommended for the social aspect.

Concerts, Art Galleries, Theater

Tickets are welcome to those who love music, dance, the stage and art displays. Again, it gives them an opportunity to share with family and friends.

Stamps, note paper, greeting cards

These are welcome since we like to keep in touch and remember old friends as well as family members. It is also wonderful to have correspondence with grandchildren, particularly when they are first learning the alphabet and beginning to print and to draw.

Gift certificates or money cards

In addition to clothing and other personal items, consider restaurants (especially those easily accessible as neighborhood venues), food markets, bus passes, etc. Basically, anything that can be used and not stored is welcome.

—◦◦◦—

Groceries

Are things hard to handle?

Is the larger, more economical size always the most economical? Remembering that we are not always as dexterous we once were, we have to be cautious as to the size and weight of purchases. For instance, a half gallon of milk may be less costly than two quarts. But it is often too heavy and so awkward to pour. The same is true of fruit juices or other liquids. Consider the size and weight of a cereal, or flour or other packaged goods.

Along with the admonitions above, there is another factor in buying the more economical large sizes of such things as meat, cheese, condiments. Will they sour or mold before we can consume them? When this happens, we are forced to toss the contents out, making us feel wasteful. We don't mind eating the same leftovers two or three days in a row, but like you, change is welcome and stimulates our lazy taste buds.

—⟨⟩⟨⟩⟨⟩—

Household Hazards

Is there anything around me that could cause me to get hurt?

The hazards occur even for those who may be in assisted living situations. The first objects to discard are small scatter rugs – in the kitchen, the bedroom, the bathroom or those scattered on top of wall-to-wall carpets. Not only do they trip but they also sometimes slide. Again, saving us from that dreadful fear of falling!

Food left to cook on the stove, tea kettle set to boil, toaster or coffee pot left plugged in, all easily forgotten. Time goes by and the smell of burned food or even a cooking utensil fills the air. The best solution, many have found, is the use of the handy dandy little kitchen timer that can be carried from room to room. Set the timer as needed, be sure it has a good, clear ring when it completes the time set, giving plenty of time to rescue whatever is in process.

Step ladders and stools invite trouble since missteps often occur, especially getting down. Avoid the two or three step ladder totally. This is an invitation to fall. However, sometimes a one step stool, if used with care, is helpful. Be sure they are large enough for a foot to be placed solidly on the top and should only be used when placed near a counter top that can be leaned upon and used for balance. Cupboards need to be arranged so dishes and utensils are reachable from the floor. The same is true of pantry areas. Bedding and towels also need lower shelves.

Winter bedding and other seasonal clothing can be stored on the higher shelves.

Know where fire alarms and smoke detectors are located and check to be sure that they are in working order at least once a month. The hearing impaired will need special smoke detection devices that have a light signal in addition to sound. There are strobe light devices available as well as vibration units for use in beds. It follows, of course, that knowing how to exit your space rapidly and easily is of paramount importance. Don't scare everyone to death, however, in discussing this need.

Men and women who have smoked cigars and cigarettes most of their lives are the most reluctant to give up this habit. It helps for the doctor to try to persuade them and for you to encourage them to quit, but nagging and threatening won't work. If smoking is not given up voluntarily, then more caution must be exercised in watching over them. There should be an absolute ban on smoking in bed or while napping on the couch. Recognizing that it is somehow a comfort occasionally, it would be wise to find designated smoking areas where the smoker lives (i.e. on the porch or patio, only in the living room - wherever it is most comfortable and less dangerous). This also requires keeping ash trays cleaned immediately to avoid any smoldering in the ashes. It also may mean rationing the tobacco daily, almost like a dose of medicine. Professional advice will help to determine what is needed for each person.

Bathroom help has been discussed under Bathing/Showers, just be aware that assistance is often needed, especially for tubs and showers. There are slipping hazards all over this room.

—◦◦◦—

Housekeeping

Am I having trouble keeping out the cobwebs?

There are many chores that become more difficult as time goes by. Making the bed, as we all know, is not a simple chore. Help would be appreciated when linens are  changed. Most of us tend to sleep in the same place every night and sometimes we almost build a nest when no changes are made. Help to rotate the mattress from time to time.

Gather a small crew of family members and scrub the bathroom down. Shower walls need cleaning, the tub thoroughly scrubbed, as well as the floor. Another crew could help clean up the kitchen cupboards, inside and out. This saves climbing up and down for those with unsteady feet and legs.

Windows need washing and blinds cleaned. It isn't that we aren't capable of doing many of these things… it is just that the strength and energy are no longer endless. We would like to have a role in doing these chores, helping the crew. Facing a complete cleaning job is too daunting and would take us forever.

Some find vacuuming a heavy chore. Moving any heavy furniture limits vacuuming to only the middle of the room so this is one area where help is definitely acceptable. The machines used may have something to do with this, but it is a housekeeping job that doesn't have to be done every day.

Don't offer to turn the place upside down and try to do it all one day. It will be difficult for us to accept too much. Let us have the opportunity to say "thank you" for the smaller chores and not feel that we are "using" our family and friends.

Each person's living circumstances will guide what help can be given. Just be aware when you are visiting to see what areas may need attention. If funds are available, hiring a housekeeping service for your *independent elderly* individual can be a real relief, even if just one time per month.

—◦◦◦—

Junk

Are my piles starting to get out of control?

Like me, many never want to throw things away. So it becomes a stack of magazines, newspapers or catalogs gathering in corners or closets. We hang onto junk mail that looks important. We save every card we receive. But, there comes a point when these stacks become a hazard, perhaps in case of fire or need of evacuation. Help us to know what the current issue is to keep. When a new one arrives, the old one goes into the recycle bin.

Clothing hanging in closets for five or ten years and never worn is welcome at many charities. The same applies to dishes, pots and pans and appliances that are no longer used. We will be more willing to let go knowing that the recycling of these items will be helping another.

—⁓—

Medicines

Am I taking my medicine properly?

Over-medication is a threat to most oldsters, particularly if they are seeing specialists in addition to the family doctor. Be sure that all doctors are on the same page as to what is being prescribed by each, including over-the-counter recommendations. It is too often a huge expense that can be reduced by this simple checking.

The handful of drugs that I was taking miraculously dwindled to a few following an emergency trip at midnight to the hospital. The cardiologist who took care of me during that episode asked immediately what medications I was taking. Fortunately, I carry a list of medications along with people to be notified, in the event something happens to me. The doctor was grateful, called my family doctor and discussed my situation. The result was that some medicine was crossed off the list, some was reduced in dosage, one was increased, and I began to return to the world.

It was after this episode that I had a new lease on life and am able to do many things that I had given up. Such things as being light-headed and dizzy, being lazy, wanting to sit or nap all the time, are all gone.

One of my helpers on this project told about the optometrist who had recommended that she take a certain vitamin which contained one substance very good for the eye problem that was starting to grow. About two weeks later, her family doctor recommended the same vitamin since it also encompassed a separate need for her that resulted from recent tests. It didn't occur at first to inquire if one pill would suffice for all needs. The answer in this case was "yes," one pill would do the job.

Ask questions about the medications. Find a friendly and knowledgeable pharmacist who will be on your side and ask questions about new prescriptions. Check with the doctor about substituting generic drugs and ask questions about why any new drugs are being prescribed. INQUIRE – INQUIRE – INQUIRE - about costs, about drug help being offered from new sources, about supplemental insurance coverage, co-pays, anything to do with finances. Sometimes the pharmacist is the best source and a good place to start these inquiries.

Another caution is the size of pills or the form other medications take. Often the prescription will require half of a pill, but the drug company does not produce tablets in that size. This necessitates cutting large pills at least in half. This often becomes a difficult task when pills are very small. Ask the doctor if the recommended pill is available in capsule or liquid form. This often helps in swallowing as well. The pharmacist is also knowledgeable about availability of other forms of medication.

Assist with dosage. It's too easy to forget time and amount. Daily medicines are more apt to be taken at the proper dosage and time of day if easy reminders are handy. A container with space for daily dosages for a week are helpful. If they are to be taken first thing in the morning or at bedtime, some reminder would be helpful here. It is important to follow instructions. Query the doctor about any side effects that may occur. Ask if they interact with other medications being taken. Read carefully all the instructions provided by the pharmacist. Some questions to ask: What are the fluid amounts to be consumed along with any pill? What time of day are they to be taken? Are they to be taken with food? Will other changes occur, such as stool habits?

Check what medical coverage each person has: Medicare, Medicaid, personal insurance perhaps carried over from retirement, supplemental coverage, and if dental, eye, or hearing coverage is included. Be certain that the primary care provider is part of the individual's "preferred" provider list for the best coverage and get a referral from the primary care provider whenever visiting a specialist. This will greatly reduce out-of-network expenses.

What do you know about the physicians, specialists, or other medical practitioners currently serving this patient? Are you satisfied with the diagnosis given? Think about second opinions. Ask questions always.

Many services have required the medical profession to limit the amount of time allowed each patient, so many are refusing to take on new patients or even giving up careers.

——✧✧✧——

Memory Loss

Am I forgetful?

Do not confuse this with Alzheimer's disease. Memory loss is not being able to readily recall someone's name although the person is recognized. It is losing words when talking. But it does not take away your life as Alzheimer's ultimately does as it wipes out a lifetime of loving, working and giving in a family. Memory loss is temporary with recall often coming within a few seconds, or later in the day.

We've all had the experience of going to another room and when we arrived, wondered what in the heck we came for. Or we have neglected to do some errand, or to attend to a special chore - you know the feeling. It is the forgetfulness that is hard. Suggest keeping a pad and pencil handy to jot things down. Need to retrieve something from the basement? Jot it down and take it when you go. A note can save making meaningless trips throughout the place.

———

Money

Am I asking for help financially when I need it?

This is especially difficult for those on limited incomes. Once all the necessities are paid each month, the little left often poses problems. Occasionally, bring shampoo or after shave, extra tissues, detergents and like products when you drop in. These all come out of the food budget so are a big help.

Little surprises add to the enjoyment of receiving these unexpected "gifts." If it is only a couple of blossoms picked on your way out of the yard, or a fresh peach or a great apple, each of you will feel blessed by the little joys given.

At the same time, we like to be able to entertain you and be the ones to pay the tab. If we ask you to have coffee and a cookie at a coffee shop once in a while, let us pay the bill. We may not be able to take you for a full course dinner at a nice restaurant but if we stop in at a fast food, at our suggestion of course, let us buy the sandwich or salad or the milkshake. Or the place may be whatever our finances may permit at any given time.

If on birthdays or at Christmas we put a few dollars into the grandkids stockings, let us do it. We need to be included and since shopping is often difficult (especially since we don't always know what each child likes and today's costs are so unreasonable) it gives us our own sense of satisfaction.

Nails, Hands and Feet

Am I taking care of my finger and toenails properly?

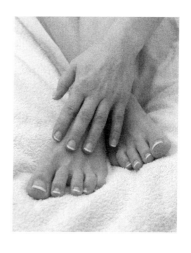

There is a tendency for nails to grow faster as one ages. They thicken and become tough, especially on the feet. It is difficult to clip toenails because of less dexterity and strength in the hands. Help is needed. A suggestion, which I have found to be a real comfort, is a trip to a podiatrist or another foot care specialist. Two or three times a year would keep feet comfortable and the cost is not prohibitive. At least the first trip is usually covered by your health care provider. The feet will often indicate other problems as well.

Keep a pumice stone on hand to use regularly on the tough skin around the heels or on a callous. Heel spurs are especially painful. An approved foot lotion should be applied regularly on rough spots. Care of the fingernails follows the practice each person is now using, but requires frequent checking concerning clipping and filing since nails chip and break more easily. Short nails are recommended, but don't discourage those who like to have longer nails - just be aware of assistance that may be needed. Manicures or pedicures as a gift occasionally will help to note when special care is needed.

Odors

How is my sense of smell?

As we age, our various senses diminish, the sense of smell being one of them. For those still living on their own, odors are often hard to detect since we live with them on a daily basis. Many of us experience urinary tract infections, so the need to be sure of body cleanliness becomes imperative. Wearing pads (or other pull-on protective garments) will save much embarrassment. Urine is one odor that is hard to disguise.

Urge a daily bathroom habit of a sponge bath to cleanse the offending places. Change undergarments daily. Keep the toilet and wash basin clean. Bidets can be one solution but costs have been high for such an installation. Recently I learned of a new bidet designed to sit on top of the existing toilet. I have been told that the cost is reasonable. Remember that if moisture accumulates on the skin in any area and is not dried and kept dry, yeast infections can occur which require a doctor's care.

—◦◦◦—

Parties

Do we enjoy them?

As we grow older, parties are sometimes more exhausting than fun. Most of us will fall into the "fun" category, however. When it comes to our own celebrations, ask us before going into extensive planning, especially where birthdays or anniversaries are concerned. Which ones would we most like to celebrate and with whom?

Many of our old friends are no longer with us. It's nice to see their children and the grandchildren but it can be overwhelming. Inviting only our own extended family and a few of any close friends remaining would the choice for many of us. Let us in on the planning, even if it is supposed to be a surprise.

—◦∞◦—

Pets

Why not?

Dogs, cats, perhaps other animals or birds, may be very old friends, and difficult to understand why they may come down to a choice no one wants to make. Strength,  mobility, cost, unexpected hazards, and where we live all come into consideration. Dogs need to be exercised and may be too big relying on strength when a leash is used. Cats often look after their own needs, but jumping up unexpectedly, or curling around feet, can be hazardous. Then there are often trips to the veterinary as they grow older along with us. The cost of medicines and the difficulty when administering are other concerns. Of course, there is also the pet food, the litter boxes, and so on. When goodbyes finally come and they are off to their own place in heaven, the harsh realization that a replacement is not the answer is a tough decision.

Many will have loved pets from whom they do not want to be parted. They offer company and consolation, like a warm body in a cold room. That makes choices even more difficult. Living conditions and mobility may ultimately make the final decision.

Bring animals to visit; especially make this a little present from grandchildren or nieces and nephews. Many assisted living places invite such visits. The opportunity to pet and love the animals, kiss them goodbye and look forward to the next visit, often brings an extra sigh of relief that we no longer have to worry about their well being.

When I first lived alone, I had a big cat that was already growing older. But I was still in the house and could let her outside. Then I moved into my present security building and could no longer let her roam free. My unit faces a busy street and at first it was a worry that when she was on the deck, she might leap over. But the traffic scared her and we were up two floors so it was a long jump. I was still working and she met me at the door every night with a welcoming meow. It was a small replacement for family. Unfortunately, about two years after we took residence, she started having problems and after about four years of trips to the veterinary, she was finally diagnosed with cancer and was in such pain that while she wanted me to hold her, it hurt too much. So when she was seventeen, I finally had to tell her goodbye and let them put her to sleep. She was the second kitty who gave me seventeen years. I could not even consider a replacement.

—⟨∿∿⟩—

Public Transportation

How can I get around town?

Many of us are still mobile enough to ride city bus lines. In most cities we also have the advantage of greatly reduced fares, which we have to apply for, of course, but well worth the effort.

Most bus drivers are courteous and careful but occasionally you get one who, either out of sorts that day or just not the right person for the job, is not so careful with the elderly or the handicapped. Most give you the courtesy of a slow entrance or exit, waiting until you are seated before starting up, and will pull the bus to the curb where it is easier for you to dismount. Encourage waiting until the bus stops before standing and be sure to use hand rails whenever available.

Buses also have lifts designed primarily for wheelchair users, but will accommodate the elderly holding several packages, with crutches or carts. It is best to utilize the bus lines during the off-peak hours, not when workers are on their way in the morning or homeward bound in late afternoon. It is not a good idea to do night traveling by bus since vision is often limited after dark and the lighting may be poor. Also, there is a high risk of being accosted on the street or on the bus in later hours and is too great to risk. Encourage the rider to not be afraid, to feel free to ask for directions or other information they may need to reach their destination.

Conductors on trains are most helpful and will look out for a traveler's welfare. Much of the same advice as given for bus lines fits here. Airlines usually have transportation to get you easily from one end of the terminal to your destination. Wherever travel takes one, the best advice is to always ask for what help is available.

—◦✦◦—

Reading Lights

Do I have sufficient light for reading?

Many of us like to read but lights are not always the best friend of the old eyes. If sitting in an easy chair to read, be sure that the lights are at the best level and at the right intensity for the reader. For those who like to read in bed, lamps are the most difficult to control. If it is a table lamp, be sure it is tall enough to shed good light on the book page. A reading lamp that fastens to the headboard might be one solution. Or the little lamps that attach to the book itself might work. If battery-powered lamps are used, be sure batteries are always available bedside. There's nothing worse than to get into the heart of a chapter you can't wait to finish and the lights go out!

Relocating

Are you suggesting that I move?

Relocating is a much kinder word than "uprooting" which is often what people feel when they are taken from their home, moved from a city or state to a strange place. There are good reasons for making the change, usually because it is easier for family to care for them (at least in the family mind); finances, of course, govern most of the decisions.

However, consider the person being moved. How long have they lived in their present situation? Is it where most of the married life was spent? Are they near markets or transportation? Are there other relatives or long time friends living in the area - perhaps one that would like to share space and living expenses? Are family buried in the city where they now live? Is the church near? These are just a few of the things to be considered.

Is there a relative or an old friend near who could keep you advised of needs or of illness, and who would willingly check regularly, by phone or dropping by?

Is it a sense of guilt that makes you believe that we need to be closer to you so that you can check us? Are you worried about bringing us into your home and how upsetting that could be?

Consider that all these thoughts are the same ones your senior person is having.

There may come a time when a move is the only solution, but as long as the health and head are reasonably good, give some careful consideration to the move.

Safety Bars

Do I have safety bars installed in my home?

The usual location for safety bars is the bathroom since this is where the majority of falls occur. The vertical bar at the toilet enables us to sit down comfortably, or to steady ourselves when standing. A hand bar at towel bar height is accommodating as we step into the tub. Other bars can be installed at shower height or along the top of the tub to assist in getting in and out.

Many can no longer use the tub for a good relaxing and sooth-ing bath, primarily because it is too difficult to get up and out. Standing in the shower can be hard if strength is a factor. Again, bars are helpful. Be sure that the tub is non-slip, either by the finish put into the new tubs or with appropriate mats. Getting in and out of the tub or the shower is where most falls occur.

Suitable chairs or benches are available so showering with a hand held device is often the answer. Remember that this is a particularly tiring project. If possible, it is a good idea to have someone present who can help if needed. Remember as well that it is difficult to give up privacy so work out a plan that will suit everyone.

Shoes/Slippers

Am I wearing the proper shoes at all times?

As we age our feet get bigger. For most of us, it is true. Because the fear of falling is always with us, it necessitates giving up heels for women, wearing more substantial shoes with solid soles for all. The problem with feet is the gradual relaxing of the arch until it becomes almost flat. The foot lengthens when this occurs and often widens as well. Spurs and callous spots occur which add to the shoe problem.

For women, all these become terrible afflictions since it means giving up the pretty shoes we all covet. It is a wonder to me that of all the great designers in the world, none have looked at the situation and given us something pretty to go with the needs of the aging foot. Shoes have been one of my passions, and having to go to "old ladies shoes" has been a terrible shock. We might as well wear hip boots with our best dresses! Men may be having the same complaint. Nevertheless, in order to keep going, we must adhere to the needs of the feet, not only for comfort, but to save those dreadful falls. It pays to have the doctor or a podiatrist determine what the need is for each. These shoes can be expensive but they wear forever. Avoid open-toed shoes and slip-ons with no back support. The tendency to wear this type of footwear only promotes the hazards of losing shoes suddenly, shuffling, tripping, and we are back to the dreaded falls.

Be aware of shoelaces not firmly tied, since loose laces can easily trip a person. Examine the soles of shoes. If they cling to carpets, a person can be pitched forward; if they are too smooth and slippery, a fall can also result. Slippers, such as bedroom slippers, should be closed at toe and heel as well. It is the same old danger of slip-ons.

Watch the stairs. Going down is most difficult since we have a tendency to catch the back of the shoe trying to be sure to use the whole stair. This can also catapult one into a fall. Going upstairs is much easier since the distance and the width of the stair is more easily discerned. Always use hand rails where available. They are more stable than a willing arm and give a feeling of strength since one is progressing at their own speed. Better still to use ramps where available.

❦

Sitting/Standing

Do you see me just falling into my chair instead of sitting down?

There are a couple of sounds one never wants to hear – "plop, plop" when an older person sits in a chair, the sofa, or the bed, and in cars, as well, because they are not sitting! They are falling into place. Notice how they back up to the place where they will be seated and literally fall backward. There comes the "plop, plop." There is an easy remedy to this if you can get them to try it out. (As you are discovering with all of this, none of us oldsters like to be told what to do. However, most of us are grateful when we do cooperate, even if it is just to please our caregiver.)

Have the person stand upright in front of the chair, holding the body upright with the legs fairly close together keeping the arms back to keep steady, then SLOWLY sit down and relax. When standing, reverse the procedure. Once on the feet, however, be sure to stand in place for a minute or so, to get the balance aligned. Rushing at any point in our lives is a "no no" because of the danger of falling. Surprisingly, the same advice applies when going to bed. Sit on the bed, as above, slightly turn to relax by the pillow and swing the legs onto the bed. There is then no danger of falling off the bed, or getting entangled in the bedding.

Avoid overstuffed sofas and chairs. They are too difficult to maneuver. Chairs should be stable, preferably with solid arms that can assist with rising.

Most agree that one of the secrets in keeping falling at bay, is positioning the legs when standing against the chair, church pew, wherever one may being seated, since it gives some direction to the space, and also helps when having to stand for a period of time. Since falling is one of the most dreaded of all happenings to the older person, any small device that helps is welcome.

Don't rush to answer the phone. Encourage standing still for a few minutes to assure they are steady. If a portable phone is available, when one sits for a time (TV viewing or reading, for instance), take the phone to the chair. Or give them the luxury of voice messaging so they won't feel they are missing something important if they don't have to hustle to answer a call.

—◆◆◆—

Talents

Do I have to give up my music or art?

Absolutely not! Just find ways to use them or share them. If singing or playing an instrument is the talent, use it to engage others in sharing as well. Is your instrument available to you? Most assisted living homes have lounges with a piano. Gather your friends there and have a sing-a-along. Play the violin or your saxophone. If drawing or painting, ask for a space where it can be carried on. If flowers are a passion, get some pots, and make them your special garden wherever they may be located. If writing is what you like to do, look into your needs for continuing this whether in your own living space or a space provided with a computer, a typewriter or a writing desk.

My mother was a soloist for her church choir and loved to sing, even when her breath didn't permit finishing a long song. The last four years of her life were in an assisted living setting. She soon found the piano in the lounge and would wander in and strike up a few notes. She played from memory and sometimes her fingers found the wrong key, but it didn't deter her. Gradually, other tenants began to drift in whenever she was there, and pretty soon she had them gathered around her singing everything from "Yankee Doodle Dandy" to "Amazing Grace," and a wide variety in between. It became almost a daily event, occasionally before lunch, often in the afternoon and, on occasion, in the evening. It encouraged others to try their almost forgotten piano skills and finally one man brought out his violin, and played along. After her death I went out occasionally to the place she had been living and found that they were still joining voices and playing their instruments.

—✑✑—

Technology

How can I easily keep in touch with the outside world?

Cordless phones are the handiest since they can be transported to any space in the living quarters. They are highly recommended since it has been established that a good percentage of falls within the home are caused by hurrying to answer a call. A good suggestion is to carry the phone even into the bathroom, in the kitchen or sitting down in an easy chair to read or watch TV. Be sure to return to the stand in the evening – these phones do need to be charged. An alternate suggestion is to furnish voice messaging which permits calls to be recorded and allows the user to check in a more timely fashion.

Cell phones are decidedly frustrating to most of us. Just instruct us how to make a call or to correctly answer when it rings. Be sure we know how to open it for use and close it when we are through. Most of us would prefer to use it just like our home phone. We don't need or care too much about all the added "benefits." We are grateful for the safety aspects provided that permits us to contact someone when we are stranded for lack of transportation or run into a problem of one sort or another while shopping. It can also enable others to use if we are in a situation where we are unable to make a call. Keep them charged as well. Be aware that many are too astute to abide by these suggestions and will want to use the phone for all the many ways it can serve. Good for them!

VHS and DVD players can be difficult to work and will most likely need a written set of basic instructions to go by. If there are more than three steps, we likely won't bother to use it. At times, family will lovingly gift us with these items when many of us feel they are fancy and too complicated for our lifestyle. The simpler the technology, the better!

The internet and e-mail can be a wonderful ways to feel connected to friends and family, but can be very intimidating. Don't feel the need to push new technology unless there is interest and be sure to take things very slow and have patience with us. Training classes are available through local libraries for beginners and I have found these classes to be quite helpful.

—◦◦◦—

The Unexpected Needs

Do I carry ID at all times?

Identification of each person should be carried at *all* times. A card or separate insertion for wallet will work. List name, address, whom to call in case of need (two people at least). Be sure the medications being taken are listed and include over-the-counter drugs as well, such as aspirin, vitamins. Note if there are drug allergies or any other type of allergy. It could save a life.

A final word... Don't smother with all the good intentions of helping. But, do teach us how to ask for that help and to do it graciously and gratefully.

A Final Note...

Information on assistance in your own area:

- State, county, city or town governments have offices to assist with senior services. They may include the availability of reduced fares on public transportation, taxi fares, utilities and rents.
- Many communities have come together to form groups for helping assist the elderly.
- Churches have established commissions to assist not only parishioners but those living in the same neighborhood.
- Investigate other social service agencies that address specific needs.
- AARP has local offices in many areas as well as the national level. They offer advice regarding assistance in almost all senior services including insurance, medical questions and assisted living locations.
- Use the internet to pursue special questions on medical problems or other help as needed.
- Don't be hesitant about using your local resources.

My Crabbèd Age

A famous novelist's spirited reflections on the sunset years
Condensed from *Today's Health*
Faith Baldwin

Yesterday my daughter presented me with a cane. This is either the beginning or the end of an era. I am, to be sure, humiliatingly unsteady, but have managed for the past five years by holding on to uncomplaining furniture, a friend or relative. I take exception to poet Robert Browning, who invited us to grow old along with him. He lived to be 77. I have sometimes wondered how he felt if, during the geriatric years, he glanced back at those lines written so much earlier.

Personally, I am tired of how-to-grow-old gracefully books. I am quite aware that there are those from 70 to 100 who crash happily about, agile as the chamois, paragons of usefulness and creativity, objects of admiration, often living efficiently alone. There are those who have survived to my age, and longer, yet appear to function without effort.

Me, I don't.

Years are all right, and survival splendid, but what these bring to us is not usually what it's cracked up to be. The books say "wisdom". Well, in my case, it's simply knowledge – everyone has to acquire a certain amount from childhood. We are expected to attain serenity – a marvelous faculty that I've not possessed since, possibly, the age of two and a half. As for becoming mellow, it sounds like something overripe.

Up until five years ago, I was merry as a grig. Then I began to receive in hospitals and examining rooms all the sensible guidelines: Be patient. adjust, accept; and one suggestion, "Just be glad you have all your buttons". (How do they know that?) I've never had a buttoned-down mind.

Pleasant people ask, "How are you able to write of contemporary matters?" This is a curious question. I am contemporary; I've always been. Everyone living in any age has to be – except the geniuses who are ahead of their eras. As I am no longer able to lurk about listening to strangers talk in planes and restaurants, nor go to parties and mind other people's vocal business, nor receive their unwitting confidences, I keep up with the times in other ways. There are basics in each generation that do not alter. And I have outside knowledge of what is known as now, thanks to radio, television, books, newspapers and magazines. It is not difficult to comprehend new mores – some of which were current in 1920. So, I have remained with today.

All I've seen and experienced has not extinguished my hopes for the world and its inheritors, the young. I wouldn't choose to be young again, but I would like to be, say, 35 and know at that age what I've learned since.

What I mind is not my age but the insistence that all is sweetness and light as one rides off into the sunset – or, more accurately, stumbles downhill. I dislike the handicaps, the figurative strait jacket, the destruction of mobility, the lessening of sight, the distressing necessity of having to look after myself but not in the tedious ways – careful of stairs, of what I eat, of drafts, of getting my feet wet.

However I must endeavor to be grateful for the buttons – and the ability to see, if through a glass darkly. I must be thankful for the power to walk at all, with or without a cane, and to hear as well as I ever have, to laugh – mostly at myself – and to enjoy such pleasures as are possible.

Of course there are sneaky, and expensive, ways to fight the battle we must eventually lose – new medication, trips to rejuvenation centers, cosmeticians, prescribed nutrition, moderate exercise, and thinking positively.

Well, I'm not fighting. I am unregenerate and lazy; all my life I've shied away from the strenuous and avoided regimens. So I'm complaining. I think it is time someone did. I can't believe I'm the only person of my age group who abhors "Brace up, you're only 80", and Browning's "The best is yet to be".

Balderdash!

I'm conscious of the fact that I'm no longer 18 and haven't been for years, except in the stubborn inner self that never grows up. I know that I cannot alter my physical disabilities, so I'll live with them – but I don't have to like it. And I do have one regret. There are so many people I'd like to meet, so many places I'd like to see.

Long ago, however, I learned to leave the table a trifle hungry. This is good discipline for the figure and, perhaps, the spirit.

———

Faith Baldwin was 83 years old when this *Reader's Digest* version was printed. She had written more than 100 books, the first in 1920, continuing to turn out at least one novel a year or an occasional short story until her death in 1978.

This condensed version is from the story published in the March 1976 issue of *Today's Health*, copyrighted 1976 by the American Medical Association. This version was printed in *Reader's Digest*.